Penalty

A Play

Stephen Smith

A Samuel French Acting Edition

SAMUELFRENCH-LONDON.CO.UK
SAMUELFRENCH.COM

Copyright © 2003 by Stephen Smith
All Rights Reserved

PENALTY is fully protected under the copyright laws of the British Commonwealth, including Canada, the United States of America, and all other countries of the Copyright Union. All rights, including professional and amateur stage productions, recitation, lecturing, public reading, motion picture, radio broadcasting, television and the rights of translation into foreign languages are strictly reserved.

ISBN 978-0-573-02359-0

www.samuelfrench-london.co.uk

www.samuelfrench.com

FOR AMATEUR PRODUCTION ENQUIRIES

UNITED KINGDOM AND WORLD EXCLUDING NORTH AMERICA

plays@SamuelFrench-London.co.uk

020 7255 4302/01

Each title is subject to availability from Samuel French, depending upon country of performance.

CAUTION: Professional and amateur producers are hereby warned that *PENALTY* is subject to a licensing fee. Publication of this play does not imply availability for performance. Both amateurs and professionals considering a production are strongly advised to apply to the appropriate agent before starting rehearsals, advertising, or booking a theatre. A licensing fee must be paid whether the title is presented for charity or gain and whether or not admission is charged.

The professional rights in this play are controlled by Samuel French Ltd, 52 Fitzroy Street, London, W1T 5JR.

No one shall make any changes in this title for the purpose of production. No part of this book may be reproduced, stored in a retrieval system, or transmitted in any form, by any means, now known or yet to be invented, including mechanical, electronic, photocopying, recording, videotaping, or otherwise, without the prior written permission of the publisher. No one shall upload this title, or part of this title, to any social media websites.

The right of Stephen Smith to be identified as author of this work has been asserted by him in accordance with Section 77 of the Copyright, Designs and Patents Act 1988

PENALTY

First performed by WCP at the Sawston Drama Festival, Cambridgeshire, on 23rd March 2002, with the following cast of characters:

Yellena Christine Easterfield
Howard Stephen Smith

Designed and directed by Mark Easterfield
Stage Managed by Julie Petrucci
with the assistance of Martin Andrus

CHARACTERS

Yellena, well-dressed; thirties
Howard, English

The action takes place in a hotel room in Baku, Azerbaijan

Time — the present

Other plays by Stephen Smith
published by Samuel French Ltd:

Background Artiste
Departure
On Location
One-Sided Triangle
Parentcraft

PENALTY

A hotel room in Baku, Azerbaijan. A summer morning

The bed is on the diagonal, with a bedside cabinet on each side; further downstage is a wardrobe, and then the door into the room. UC is a small table, and L are two chairs, one each side of a door to the bathroom. The "fourth wall" is a wide window

As the CURTAIN *rises, the bedside radio is playing something suitably Eastern European. The room is almost dark, lit only by the spill from a sliver of daylight which falls across the bed and reveals Howard deep in slumber*

Yellena, a well-dressed girl in her thirties, enters with a breakfast tray and places it on the table. She mimes opening the curtains on the "fourth wall", flooding the room with light. Howard groans loudly and tries to hide his head under the blanket. Yellena switches off the radio and gives a gentle cough

Yellena Mr Robertson ... Mr Robertson ... is morning.

Howard groans again

   You ask me to wake you at seven.

He groans again, but begins to move

   Is Yellena from ministry.
Howard (*peering up from under the pillow*) Oh ...
Yellena (*pointing to the table*) I have breakfast.

Howard (*beginning to sit up*) Hmm?
Yellena Tea and muffins.
Howard Oh ... Yellena!
Yellena Typical English breakfast, no.
Howard (*trying to wake himself up*) Oh my head ...
Yellena (*at the table*) Shall I be mother? (*She pours out the tea*)
Howard What happened last night?
Yellena Welcome dinner.
Howard Oh yes.
Yellena PG Tips. (*She offers him the cup, then puts it on the bedside cabinet*)
Howard Thank you.
Yellena Milk from cow ... Pills for head. (*She proffers him a bottle of pills*)
Howard Thanks. (*He tackles the pill bottle*)
Yellena Home from home, no?
Howard Sort of.
Yellena Marmalade or jam?
Howard Perhaps a bit later. I'm not very hungry at the moment.
Yellena Cucumber sandwiches?
Howard What?
Yellena With corners off. I can get.
Howard No thanks, the tea will do fine.
Yellena Good.

She watches him drink his tea

Good?
Howard Yes.
Yellena (*poised with the teapot*) Shall I be mother again?
Howard No thanks, one is enough.
Yellena (*putting the teapot back on the tray*) Last night you drink like fish.
Howard (*shocked*) Really! I don't remember.
Yellena Is correct?
Howard No, it isn't. I hardly drink at home — that's why it must have gone straight to my head.

Yellena No — is correct to say "drink like fish"?
Howard It is, if I did.
Yellena Is strange thing to say, no? How do you know how fish drink?
Howard It's because fish swim with their mouths open, so it looks as if they are drinking all the time.
Yellena Ah I see, and "eat like horse" is because horse run with mouth open, no?
Howard No. (*He realizes he is only wearing a T-shirt and boxer shorts under the sheets*) What exactly happened to my clothes?
Yellena (*taking the* UL *chair from its place and putting it by the table*) My mother has them.
Howard Your mother!
Yellena (*sitting and taking her tea*) Cannot trust hotel manager from Dagestan.
Howard Right and ... er ... (*worried*) why has your mother got my clothes?
Yellena Sick as a fish last night.
Howard Your mother?
Yellena You. Straight from horse's mouth. Go everywhere.
Howard (*embarrassed*) All over my clothes?
Yellena And mayor, wife of mayor, daughter of mayor, and my dog.
Howard My God.
Yellena No ... my dog.
Howard (*disbelieving*) I was sick over the mayor last night.
Yellena Do not worry, few years ago Yeltsin he come and sick over mayor too.
Howard What about my colleagues?
Yellena They sit next to deputy mayor.
Howard Were they sick?
Yellena No.
Howard Drunk?
Yellena Sing a little.
Howard (*looking around*) What about the rest of my clothes?
Yellena With my mother.

Howard As well!
Yellena Problem with police. Search suitcase, make terrible mess, my mother not happy. She say Englishman think Azerbaijan very dirty country. I say Azerbaijan is dirty country, she say, not point, "seeing is believing".
Howard Your mother is very profound.
Yellena And have cleaning business.
Howard Why were the police searching my suitcase?
Yellena Because you arrive five hours late at airport, customs men go home. We take you straight to welcome banquet, police have to search suitcase. Is Azeri way.
Howard What were they looking for?
Yellena Vodka.
Howard It's illegal to bring in vodka?
Yellena No, but most people put inside vodka for quick time through customs.
Howard Oh I see, and they roughed up my clothes because there was no vodka.
Yellena They say case not close properly. Angry to wait for nothing.
Howard Do they know why I'm here?
Yellena Police law unto themselves.
Howard That's very reassuring.
Yellena No problem. If police cause trouble, mayor send tank.
Howard The mayor still likes me then.
Yellena Not care about weak stomach last night as long as have strong stomach tonight.
Howard Oh I see.
Yellena You think you have strong stomach tonight?
Howard I hope so.
Yellena So do we.
Howard Good.
Yellena (*standing sharply*) Is very important we beat the Russian bastards.
Howard (*quickly changing the subject*) So what am I going to do about clothes?

Yellena Mother bring clothes soon.
Howard And I have to wait in bed until she comes.
Yellena If you like.
Howard Well I can hardly waltz down to reception like this!
Yellena You want to waltz?
Howard Figure of speech. I mean I can't walk about the hotel like this.
Yellena (*standing at the window*) Can admire lovely view. Baku very beautiful city despite Russian bastards building concrete monsters everywhere. Still have old city with ancient mosques, museums, galleries and parks. Come and look.
Howard (*reluctant*) Well ...
Yellena I can get tablecloth?
Howard No ... no it's all right — I can use this. (*He wraps a bedcover round himself and joins her at the window*)
Yellena You see that is Old City. Beautiful, yes? Stalin, he plan to destroy all this.
Howard Why didn't he?
Yellena Too busy destroying other things.
Howard (*pointing*) What's that tower with no windows?
Yellena Is called Maiden Tower.
Howard Reminds me of where I used to work. A windowless tower full of bureaucracy.
Yellena (*surprised*) You used to work in tower like this?
Howard Well it had windows, but you couldn't open them or it upset the air conditioning.
Yellena This was built by daughter of Baku ruler.
Howard Ours was built by the council too.
Yellena She was so beautiful her own father fall in love with her. Afraid of what her father might do, she get him to build tower to keep busy. She say she want to see all his land. Every time they finish she ask for one more floor. When they can build no higher she climbs to the top and jumps off.
Howard Killing herself?
Yellena Yes, for shame of what father might do.
Howard When was this?

Yellena About eight hundred years ago. My grandfather, he tell me this story. (*She laughs*) So probably not true.
Howard It certainly is a very good view.
Yellena Over there is Caspian Sea. Have big promenade, big park. (*Suddenly serious*) I used to play as child until Russian soldier rape me. Then I play no more.
Howard I'm sorry.
Yellena Is not your fault. At time I think perhaps good idea I get someone build me maiden tower but I am no longer maiden.
Howard (*gently*) Is that why you hate the Russians so much?
Yellena Not only rape me but rape all country. One hundred years ago we were biggest producer of oil in world. Red Army march in, take oil, stir up trouble with neighbours. Only leave a few years ago. You know Baku means "City Bitten by Wind". The wind she comes from Russian Steppes across Caspian Sea. Even now we still cannot stop Russia torturing us. To little proud nation, the smallest of victories makes the harshest of winters more bearable. We can keep warm with talk of great day we gave Russian bear bloody nose.
Howard Yes ...
Yellena Old memories still fresh. Opportunity to create new memories very important. If win we will know truly independent. Can hold head high in world.
Howard I don't think one football match is going to change the past.
Yellena When England win World Cup whole country happy yes?
Howard Yes.
Yellena Azeri team beat Russian team then whole of Azerbaijan happy.
Howard It's not exactly the same.
Yellena Is better. Not only beat Russians but have first Azerbaijan team in Champions League. Manchester United, Real Madrid, Juventus come to Baku.
Howard (*looking out of the window and desperately trying to change the subject*) Where's that ship going to?
Yellena Is ferry to Turkmenistan. Lucky you don't go there, very smelly peoples.

Howard Is there any nationality that you do like?
Yellena (*looking at him and smiling*) I like English.
Howard Ah.
Yellena (*touching his legs*) Have to have strong legs to be referee. Run around for ninety minutes. Maybe longer if have extra time.
Howard (*pulling away*) Speaking of which what happened to my kit?
Yellena Black bag?
Howard Yes.
Yellena In bathroom.
Howard Didn't rough up that then.
Yellena No. Police have respect for uniform.
Howard I've got some shorts in there, might as well put them on for the time being.
Yellena Good idea.

Howard goes into the bathroom

Yellena pours them both another cup of tea

Howard (*off, from the bathroom*) Are my colleagues next door?
Yellena Next door?
Howard In the next rooms?
Yellena Not in hotel.
Howard What do you mean not in the hotel. Where are they?
Yellena Smaller hotel in old city. Number one man have best hotel in Baku, number twos must have number two hotel. Is problem?

Howard enters wearing black shorts

Howard (*becoming increasingly agitated*) But we're all supposed to be in the same hotel.
Yellena Is not Azeri way.
Howard But it's the UEFA way.
Yellena Too late now. Tonight you go home, yes.
Howard Yes, but we've still got to be together.

Yellena Tonight of course.
Howard No, this morning when we go to inspect the ground.
Yellena Is not possible. Is closed this morning. Today is Army Day. Is why we have big party last night, not just because you come.
Howard It can't be closed for us. We have to do a mandatory inspection.
Yellena Is very important day.
Howard That doesn't matter.
Yellena Very important day. Normally peoples he celebrate all day but today stadium officials go back to work in afternoon. For this we must be truly thankful.
Howard So we can't visit the stadium until this afternoon?
Yellena After meet your colleagues for lunch. Do not worry, plenty to do. I take you see city when my mother brings clothes. Your wish is my command.
Howard What about the match observer?
Yellena Is Polish, won't see him until lunchtime. (*She thrusts a cup of tea into his hand*)
Howard This is all very irregular. (*He sits in the chair next to the table*)
Yellena We have beautiful carpets. (*Sitting on the edge of the bed with her tea*)
Howard I'm sure you do.
Yellena Best designs in world. Can have carpet with your name or even photo inside.
Howard I'm sure my wife would love that, then she can literally walk all over me.
Yellena Ah, you are under thumb.
Howard Not exactly.
Yellena Your wife is pretty?
Howard Yes, I suppose so.
Yellena But beauty isn't everything.
Howard No, but it helps if you've got to look at her for the rest of your life.
Yellena You expect to stay with her for life?
Howard Isn't it what marriage is supposed to be about?

Yellena Still love her?
Howard Why all the questions?
Yellena Curious how other peoples live.
Howard I've got a picture in ... (*wondering where his wallet is*) where's my wallet?
Yellena In your bag. I empty jacket and put everything in bag.
Howard Thanks.

Howard goes into the bathroom to get his bag

Yellena (*tidying the cups and coming* D) I expect you also have many handsome childrens.
Howard (*off*) Two boys.

Howard returns with his bag, and sits on the bed rummaging for his wallet

I don't know how I let myself get into such a state. Nothing like this has ever happened to me before.
Yellena Is very strong drink if you are not used to it.
Howard Must have been. God knows what my colleagues think.
Yellena Do not worry nobody knows except us. You were on separate table at different end of hall and left before end.
Howard Do you know I can't remember a thing.
Yellena Is your first match, yes?
Howard In the middle at senior international level, yes, although of course I've been the fourth official — speaking of which, is the fourth official in a fourth-rate hotel?
Yellena We have no fourth-rate hotels in Baku.
Howard Good.
Yellena We put him in third-rate hotel.
Howard (*standing*) You know I'm going to have to write a report about this.
Yellena You being drunk.
Howard No — the fact we are all in separate hotels. I can't keep it quiet.

Yellena No problem. Is not my decision.
Howard Did you treat the officials in the previous round the same?
Yellena They were Romanians.
Howard So?
Yellena I don't speak Romanian. Was nothing to do with me.
Howard Is this your first international match?
Yellena For football. You were going to show me picture of wife.
Howard Yes. (*He gets it out of his wallet*)
Yellena Very pretty.
Howard Are you married?
Yellena No.
Howard Engaged?
Yellena No. I work long hours and live with family.
Howard Career girl. No time for a social life.
Yellena We are Muslim, women do not go out at night. Is man's world.
Howard I see. I thought Muslims weren't supposed to drink alcohol?
Yellena Depends how you read Koran. Says we must not drink wine and we do not — but says nothing about vodka. You have pictures of sons?
Howard Yes. (*He hands them to her*) Patrick's eight and Roger is twelve.
Yellena Handsome like father.
Howard I don't know about that.
Yellena (*looking at him*) I do.
Howard (*slightly rattled*) That's very kind of you ... Perhaps, I'd better put my socks on! (*He sits on the bed, takes his socks and trainers from his bag and starts to put them on*) They certainly don't take after their father. Very academic like their mother. Instead of kicking a football about they've always got their heads buried in books.
Yellena Is not bad thing.
Howard No — it's just there's more to life than education. Personal experiences can teach you a lot more about yourself than any book can.

Yellena Your wife, she teacher?
Howard Head teacher now.
Yellena Very clever.
Howard Cleverer than me.
Yellena Married long time?
Howard Fifteen years.
Yellena Here have to wait until after Ramadan to get married. When bride gets to groom's home is led three times around stove and must crush plate with heel.
Howard She doesn't get to walk over a carpet with his photo in it then?
Yellena No. Also must have head of sheep on path to wedding as sign of good luck.
Howard Not for the sheep.
Yellena How you get married?
Howard Registry office. We aren't really religious. We didn't have a lot of money, so we spent our honeymoon on the Isle of Wight.
Yellena Is hot, Isle of Wight?
Howard No, but my wife had friends there who lent us their cottage.
Yellena For Christians, Azerbaijan was important place. Near Tabriz, which is now in Iran, was Garden of Eden from bible. And Noah's Ark he crash here after great flood. Five thousand years ago carve great gash in Snake Mountain. Is why white people are called Caucasian. Azerbaijan is in Caucasus and first white people come from Noah's Ark.
Howard (*standing and joining her*) Is that true?
Yellena How do I know? I'm Muslim.
Howard Would have made more sense if Noah's Ark had crashed into the Isle of Wight.

They both laugh

Yellena Is great experience for me to talk to westerner, to improve English and learn about new places like Isle of Wight.
Howard I think the Garden of Eden beats the Isle of Wight hands down.

Yellena "Hands down" — that's good. I have another phrase. I love to discover your sayings. You have noticed.
Howard Yes. I'm amazed at the amount you know.
Yellena I read every English book I can find from Jeffrey Archer to P.G. Wodehouse.
Howard That does cover quite a spectrum.
Yellena Very clever man.
Howard Jeffrey Archer?
Yellena No. P.G. Wodehouse. Very funny and can make tea too. Most of all I like sayings that rhyme like silly billy or fiddle faddle. Please, what is faddle?
Howard No idea.
Yellena I cannot find in my dictionary. Is very frustrating when only understand one half of phrase. For example I know what is willy, but why is it nilly?
Howard I've gone through life without knowing, so I shouldn't let it bother you.
Yellena But I want to impress.
Howard Don't worry, you're doing that already.
Yellena I love my country but I want to travel, to see world — instead of walking three times around stove and crush plate with heel.
Howard I understand.
Yellena You do?
Howard Yes.
Yellena Azeri man would never understand. He only want food on table and wife for making childrens.
Howard But you don't have a man so does that matter?
Yellena Is not simple. If I leave country and find life better in West, how can I come back and live as Azeri woman again.
Howard You might not find life better in the West. You might want to come back because you prefer your old life.
Yellena You have spare room in house?
Howard Pardon?
Yellena If I come to England can I stay at your house?
Howard It's not very big.

Yellena You haven't seen my house. I share room with mother.
Howard On holiday you mean?
Yellena I could help your wife with housework and cook food.
Howard (*beginning to panic*) I thought that's what you wanted to avoid.
Yellena Sorry we do not "beat around bush", we say what we think, not tactful like English, but take no offence if answer no.
Howard No, I didn't say no, you just caught me by surprise. Of course if you ever were in England we'd be happy to put you up for a few nights.
Yellena Problem I don't have much money so who knows when, but if I have address of Englishman makes easier for visa.
Howard (*feeling uneasy*) Right, I see. Er — do you know when your mother might be coming with my clothes?
Yellena Soon.
Howard Good because I think the sightseeing trip would be a good thing to do. Broaden my horizons and all that.
Yellena Have you ever been unfaithful to your wife?
Howard (*shocked*) You *do* believe in saying what you think. (*He sits on the end of the bed*)
Yellena If you were Russian already you would try have sex with me.
Howard Really!
Yellena All they think about. You see Russian women very ugly. So they make excuse for business trips but only want sex. Is very difficult to be interpreter.
Howard Don't people speak Russian here?
Yellena We had to under Soviet Union but since independence we have pride. Why should we talk to Russian in Russian when they will not learn Azeri. Is why I work hard with English, I don't want to talk to Russian. I want to talk to Englishman or American. Problem not many come so sometimes I get Russian.
Howard And they make sexual advances?
Yellena Always. Sometimes ask for photo of interpreter. Is why today is great day for me. To be with honourable Englishman. To have good "chinwag".

Howard Well, you'll have no problems from me.
Yellena You do not find me attractive?
Howard No, I didn't mean that. I meant you'll have no unwelcome advances.

Yellena moves and sits next to him on the bed and puts her hand on his knee

Yellena So if I welcome, you advance?
Howard No, I didn't mean that either. I meant I'm a married man.
Yellena (*beginning to stroke his leg*) So?
Howard So I must remain faithful to my wife.
Yellena Must?
Howard Yes.
Yellena You say sometimes better to experience life than just read books.

The stroking has become rather too much for Howard

Howard (*hurriedly getting up*) Yes but ——
Yellena Nobody will know. Tonight you will be gone never to return. We will be "two ships that pass in night" — except will be daytime.
Howard I thought you didn't like men propositioning you?
Yellena Not Russians who have nothing to offer except few roubles and vodka. Is different with Englishman who have spare room. (*She pats the bed enticingly*)
Howard I couldn't have you coming to my house if I'd slept with you.
Yellena Why not? Perhaps we can again when your wife she goes to Bingo.
Howard My wife wouldn't be seen dead at Bingo.
Yellena Or we meet at football ground. Every Saturday you go to big football ground in England, perhaps stay night in hotel ...
Howard No, no, you've got me all wrong, I'm not like that.
Yellena (*after a pause*) Except when drunk?
Howard What?

Penalty

Yellena You know KGB use this hotel in Soviet time? They use for honey-trap. You know honey-trap? Have woman sleep with man ——
Howard I know what a honey-trap is.
Yellena Have secret camera. Is still used.
Howard By whom?
Yellena Government.
Howard As a honey-trap?
Yellena If necessary.
Howard How do you know?
Yellena I work for Government. (*She gets up*) You know we lose 2-1 in Moscow. So if win 1-0 tonight go to next round.
Howard On the away goals rule, yes.
Yellena Is no secret that Russians get help from referee.
Howard I'm sorry but I don't believe that.
Yellena Is from Bulgaria, Bulgarians always do what Russians ask. Russians ask for late penalty, and as sure as eggs is eggs, Russians get penalty in eighty-ninth minute. All we ask is for same. Fair treatment for both sides.
Howard I'm sorry but I think we should stop this conversation before you say something you may regret.
Yellena All we ask is for same. What is good for goose is good for gander.
Howard That's how I intend it to be. Same treatment for both sides no matter what allegedly happened in the first leg. To me it's just two sets of colours.
Yellena You know all Russians ask is for late penalty. Very easy for referee at corner. Lot of pushing. Most times referee he turns blind eye, true?

Howard does not answer

But sometimes he thinks this is bit worse and gives penalty. Everyone cry, "what for?" He signals with hand, "pushing". Defence not happy, but accept, have seen before. Perhaps Baku not need help of referee. I hope so. I pray so. All we want is insurance.

Howard (*going to the door*) I think it's best you leave.
Yellena You know, I try very hard to make you like me.
Howard I do, but please don't ask me to do something you know I can't.
Yellena Perhaps even feel sorry for me as underdog.
Howard Don't do this, please.
Yellena I try very hard not to have to tell you but you leave no alternative. Camera, he film you last night. With two girls. Make look like you have good time.
Howard What two girls?
Yellena You are nice man. I do not like to do this. I even try offer myself, if you love me you help me, but no, love wife too much.
Howard What two girls?
Yellena You see, I love my country too much, have one chance to do big thing for my country.
Howard I don't remember anything about two girls.
Yellena Put pill in drink. Have video and photos. Send to newspapers if have to.
Howard Who are you working for?
Yellena You may think no referee bribed or blackmailed but we sure he was in Moscow and all we want is same. One penalty.
Howard And what if I tell the match observer before the game?
Yellena Then how you say, "shit hit fan". Big problems for both of us.
Howard Not for me.
Yellena Of course for you. Tell UEFA you sleep with two girls before game and get blackmailed, they will not trust you again. Is end of international games.
Howard But I didn't consciously.
Yellena Is what is called "no smoke without fire", yes? Is good story for newspapers, especially with photos. Is not good for family to see.
Howard It's also not very good for your club.
Yellena Club he know nothing. I act on own and will be punished, not club.
Howard But you aren't acting on your own?

Yellena Soldiers get shot and generals walk away. We are both soldiers.
Howard But this isn't a war.
Yellena Not to you. But to me very serious. Is more important than job.
Howard Refereeing is more than a job. I'm not going to jeopardize it for anything.
Yellena Not even for marriage?
Howard No, not even for that. Look you've made a big mistake trying that on with me. You've picked on totally the wrong person.
Yellena But you said how much you love wife.
Howard I didn't. You did. My wife couldn't care less what I get up to abroad. In fact I'm the family joke, I think they're pleased I'm out of the house so much. My wife and kids gave up on me years ago. When we got married Anne thought it'd be easy to get me to give up football. She hates it — she thinks I should have achieved much more instead of traipsing around the country in search of abuse. I shouldn't be here, I should be doing some Open University course in brain surgery. I've got two egghead sons without a sporting bone in their bodies and a wife who only sleeps with me if she's had a good Ofsted report. You know what the worst thing about all this is? For the first time ever I'm in bed with two girls and I can't remember a thing about it.
Yellena So you want me to get friend? So this time you can remember?
Howard No, of course not.
Yellena Why not?
Howard It's not marriage to my wife that's important, it's my marriage to football.
Yellena Your marriage to football?
Howard However beautiful you are, Yellena, I'm not throwing away twenty years of my life for twenty minutes of lust. I've emerged from dodging cowpats in the middle of nowhere to walking out in front of sixty thousand at Old Trafford — and I'm not going to sacrifice that for anything.
Yellena But you don't have to. Will be our secret. Like last night.

Howard How can it be a secret when there are other people involved?

Yellena Is no chance you will come here again so doesn't matter if they know. Why will they say anything if we get penalty. I promise destroy video and photos after game. Then no proof. No-one can ever find out.

Howard Except before the game you up the ante to disallowing any goals the opponents score. I'm not stupid. One penalty won't guarantee victory.

Yellena Is not your problem. We are honourable. A deal is a deal.

Howard An honourable blackmailer! — that is novel. Sorry, but you give me no option but to report this.

Yellena And say what?

Howard That I'm being blackmailed.

Yellena And how do you prove it. I will deny everything. I will say you have drunken dream. Your colleagues he will confirm you leave party early, drunk. Look, is very easy, no-one needs to know.

Howard But I will, and if it comes out that I've cheated, every controversial decision I've ever made will no longer be a genuine mistake but corruption. I haven't got much to show for my life, and you're asking me to wipe it all out for a country I'd never even heard of a few weeks ago. If I'm going to be a soldier killed in battle, I'd prefer it to be for the right reasons.

Yellena Then we have stalemate.

Howard No we don't because there's no way I'm walking on to that pitch with a blackmail threat hanging over my head. Look, just give me the tape and we'll forget all about it.

Yellena (*becoming agitated*) I cannot do that.

Howard Then I will be ill. I'll get food poisoning. I'll pull a muscle. The fourth official will have to take over.

Yellena Then they will definitely release tape.

Howard Which will prove I've been blackmailed.

Yellena And destroy personal life.

Howard For me it would be worse to be found cheating on the pitch than in bed.

Yellena crumples into the DL *chair, and buries her head in her hands*

Yellena They will hurt family.
Howard Who will?

Yellena turns away but he goes up to her

Who will hurt your family?
Yellena I cannot say.
Howard (*after a pause*) Are you being blackmailed? (*He pauses again while he digests this thought*) You're being blackmailed too, aren't you ...? Look, tell me who it is and perhaps I can help.
Yellena Only one way you can help.
Howard This hasn't got anything to do with hating Russia has it?

Yellena doesn't answer

It's about money, isn't it? The millions that will come Baku's way if they get into the Champions league. That's what this is all about isn't it?
Yellena (*in tears*) Please they will kill my father.
Howard Who? Someone at the Club?
Yellena No, no, this not football people.
Howard Then who?
Yellena You can do nothing. All you can do is give me penalty. Please. If you do that, I have done job, they release father.
Howard Until the next game.
Yellena I don't care. Once game is over we leave Baku, go back to Russia.
Howard (*shocked*) Back to Russia?
Yellena My parents are Russian. They come here for oil. My father he works in oil business until independence, then he lose job.
Howard (*bewildered*) I don't understand. You have just spent the last half hour telling me how evil the Russians are and now you tell me *you* are one.
Yellena Not me. My parents. I was born here.
Howard So you don't hate the Russians?

Yellena I don't hate anybody. I love my country. I love my parents' country. Is trick to make you hate them. They tell me do this. What choice do I have?
Howard Go to the police?
Yellena I tell you I have no choice.
Howard So someone blackmails you and you then blackmail me. It's a circle of violence that has to be stopped somewhere.
Yellena It will finish this evening. Either Baku have penalty or my father dies.
Howard How can I believe anything you tell me — ever since we've met you've been telling me a pack of lies.
Yellena I tell you truth about Russia but I cannot hate people I have same blood with.
Howard Are you a Muslim?
Yellena No.
Howard (*angry*) So it is all lies.
Yellena (*standing*) No! Is true about Russian soldier on promenade, is true about Russian businessmen. (*Angrily approaching him*) You think is easy to be me. Russians treat me like Azeri, Azeris treat me like Russian. My father lose job, my mother she can only do cleaning, my brother killed in Armenia, so I have to support family. When he have job my father spend lot of money to send me to school, how can I desert him now? Is true I want to leave, is true I want to see West but first I have to help family. Then if I get job in West I can help family even more.
Howard These people have kidnapped your father?
Yellena Yes.
Howard And threatened to kill him if Baku don't win?
Yellena If Baku do not have penalty.
Howard Irrespective of the score?
Yellena All they want is penalty. Can be any time.
Howard (*surprised*) It doesn't matter if they don't win? Why?
Yellena Is gambling, is very big gambling.
Howard But not on the result.
Yellena They gamble on anything. What time first goal, what time first corner ...
Howard What time Baku get a penalty?

Penalty

Yellena Or if there is penalty or not.
Howard And they found out you will be looking after the match officials and held your father to ransom.
Yellena They tell me to convince you to give penalty to Baku. Up to me how but if doesn't happen then my father dead.
Howard And you're sure they'll kill him?
Yellena Is not worth gamble. They are very big organization. Gambling, prostitution, smuggling, they control everything.
Howard Which means if they know for sure there will be a penalty in the game they can make a lot of money.
Yellena From people who bet Baku will not have penalty.
Howard And these two girls were prostitutes?

A pause. She sits on the bed

Yellena Is no two girls.
Howard No video?
Yellena No.
Howard Nothing happened?
Yellena No.
Howard Nothing at all?
Yellena Sorry, is only way I could think to help father without hurting anyone else.
Howard But you were prepared to wreck my family, my career …
Yellena How with no video? Was all bluff. Is no camera.
Howard Thank God. (*He sits in the* DL *chair and breathes a sigh of relief*) But I was drunk.
Yellena Pill not work well. Make you sick everywhere so I have to give you another one to make unconscious.
Howard You could have killed me!
Yellena No, is safe. Is what prostitutes use to rob fat Russians and not have sex with them. Is female version what Americans call date rape except is date rob.
Howard And you've done this before?
Yellena No — at work I see story on CNN and ask friend if happen in Baku. She tell me what to do. Is first time, is why I get pills wrong. I am sorry but when desperate have to do desperate things.

Your head, he is all right now?
Howard (*smiling*) Yes he is. I suppose my colleagues are not in separate hotels and my clothes are not with your mother.
Yellena Your clothes are downstairs.
Howard And my colleagues?
Yellena Next door. (*Pause*) You want I should leave now?
Howard What about your father?

Yellena simply looks away

Surely the police must be able to do something?
Yellena What police?
Howard You must have police.
Yellena We do, but my father is in Russia.
Howard They kidnapped your father in Russia?
Yellena Went to see his brother who is ill in Rostov last week. They take him in street, throw in back of car and no-one see again. My uncle he gets photo and instructions for me.
Howard So this is nothing to do with Azerbaijan?
Yellena Is Russian mafia. They join with syndicates in Asia to control lot of big gambling. Many football matches, horse races, any sport.
Howard I have to report this, you know.
Yellena Only if they kill my father — *please*. (*She comes to him imploringly*) While he is alive I cannot risk his life.
Howard So you want me to go on to the pitch knowing that if I don't give a penalty your father could be killed.
Yellena Please.
Howard What if I don't do the game?
Yellena Does not matter who is referee is penalty they want. (*She takes a photo out of her pocket*) This is my father. Is handsome man, proud man, but life has not been good to him. One time, when I was child, we have good house, good clothes but now we are poor and he can do nothing.
Howard Whatever happens after the match you still intend to leave Baku?
Yellena My mother has already gone to Rostov hoping she will see

my father again.
Howard But it's nothing to do with Azerbaijan.
Yellena Must never happen again. I cannot risk family with this job.
Howard I shouldn't think things are much better in Russia.
Yellena We can stay with family in Rostov. Perhaps I find job on farm.
Howard With your language skills.
Yellena (*moving away from Howard*) Is too dangerous to use. Is safer to be peasant.
Howard It would be such a waste. (*He pauses, then rises*) Look perhaps I could find out if there is any chance of you coming to England.
Yellena To stay with you?
Howard To study, perhaps get a translating job. Must be a demand for someone who can speak Russian, Azeri and English.
Yellena Will I be with you?
Howard I don't know. I can't make any promises. It might not be possible.
Yellena Finally I make you feel sorry for me.
Howard No, it's not pity. (*Pause*) If you are not Muslim what are you?
Yellena I was Communist, we had no religion.
Howard What are you now?
Yellena Capitalist and still have no religion, why?
Howard I was going to get you to swear on the Bible or the Koran or something.
Yellena I will swear on my father's life.
Howard He might be dead already, you know.
Yellena I would know. (*Hopefully*) You believe I am telling truth?
Howard I hope so, or I'm going to look the biggest idiot that walked the earth. You didn't have to tell me about the video ... so ... I'll do what I can.
Yellena You are going to give penalty?
Howard (*very hesitantly throughout*) There are seventeen laws of the game, but sometimes referees add an eighteenth which we call common sense. I sure as hell don't want your father's death on my conscience but I can't compromise my impartiality. They want

Baku to have a penalty, but that doesn't stop me giving one to Moscow as well. Hopefully Baku will get a genuine penalty, but if they don't I can be stricter in the penalty area than normal and if it has a fundamental affect on the scoreline then I can be equally harsh in the other box. But it certainly won't make me very popular.

Yellena (*her Azerbaijan accent suddenly gone*) No, it won't. (*Getting out a small notebook from her pocket and writing*) In my opinion five out of ten is the best you'll get. Although of course, the final decision is not up to me.

As Yellena has said these words, we see first surprise, then incomprehension across Howard's face. There is a pause as he digests what he has heard

Howard (*turning sharply towards her*) What the ...

Yellena Of course the golden rule is never get separated from your colleagues. Once that happens you are open to all types of coercion, blackmail, heartbreaking stories. Safety in numbers is the golden rule.

Howard (*stunned*) What?

Yellena Your assessment. Five out of ten. You'll have it in writing in two weeks.

Howard My assessment? (*Suddenly very angry*) My assessment! This has all been a bloody assessment!

Yellena Look — officials have been bribed in the past, and with the Champions League the financial temptations are even greater. So UEFA now does selective role-play scenarios to test and train its new intake of senior officials.

Howard I've been put through hell and then you calmly say it's a training exercise. This isn't the bloody SAS. We're football referees, not undercover agents.

Yellena We don't *want* undercover agents, because the one overriding quality every official must have is honesty and we have no shortage of candidates so we can select the cream.

Howard I don't believe this.

Penalty 25

Yellena At home all you have to worry about is the game, but at international level, with maybe millions at stake, it is a totally different ballgame. You are in charge, you are responsible for your colleagues in a strange land.
Howard (*angrily*) I know that.
Yellena Then why am I here with you alone? Why have I engineered a scenario in which you are prepared to break the rules?
Howard Because you spiked my drink.
Yellena And I wouldn't have been able to if your colleagues had been seated at the same table. Instead you let me lead you across to the other side of the room out of sight of your team.
Howard I didn't want to offend you.
Yellena You're a referee, not a diplomat on a goodwill mission. Let the match observer sort out the niceties with the local officials. Be guided by him.
Howard He wasn't at the airport!
Yellena Then you should have waited for him. You do not go off with just the interpreter. If no-one else shows, you phone UEFA headquarters and wait for instructions.
Howard (*dejected*) So I'm finished. I'm finished before it's even started.
Yellena If you had accepted any sexual or financial favours we'd be on our way to Baku airport by now. However you received ten marks for refusing to alter the final result despite emotional blackmail but lost five for being prepared to give an undeserved penalty because of the emotional blackmail. Of course it does mean that if you don't achieve high marks on the pitch throughout the season then you will be off. It's a harsh world out there, there's no room for nice guys.
Howard So I'm still in the middle tonight?
Yellena If you feel up to it. Otherwise you can swap places with the fourth official and we can give you an imaginary injury. Of course you'd have to consent to us using the video for training.
Howard What video?
Yellena (*going to the wardrobe and retrieving a small video*

camera which has been hidden on top under some spare blankets) The one that's been used to film this entire episode. (*She switches it off*) We need it for your assessment report and security reasons but they also make useful training videos.

Howard I've been treated like an imbecile and then you want to show it to all my colleagues!

Yellena It's not for your colleagues, it's for training people like me.

Howard And exactly who are you?

Yellena A formerly under-employed actress who's found a career in role-play with UEFA. Look — we're not out to get you, unless you are corrupt. You're a nice bloke but a little too trusting. In the long run I hope I've helped you to avoid getting into something like this for real. Be a blot on my copybook if you quit now.

Howard I don't know. At the moment I'm feeling very disillusioned and frankly very embarrassed. I thought I was talking to a total stranger and I said — well I said things I shouldn't have said. Stuff I've never told anyone.

Yellena There's no need to feel embarrassed, it was a very difficult scenario, I laid it on with a trowel, only a heartless thug wouldn't have been affected. Your arrival in the country is the start of the match. Always be in control.

Howard (*coming close to her*) You know, for a few moments I —

Yellena (*gently, stopping him going further*) I have to go now. I've done my job and I'll leave you to do yours.

Howard (*shocked*) That's it?

Yellena Yes. I've said all I have to. I'll make sure your clothes are sent up, and you'll get a written report in the post... you won't be seeing me again.

Howard But...

Yellena (*smiling*) No buts. (*She shakes his hand*) Enjoy the match.

Yellena exits

Howard Enjoy the match?

He stares at the door, then slowly sits on the bed, uncertain what to do next. He sees his holdall, picks it up and then begins to take out his referee's shirt. He looks at the shirt, remembering why he wanted to be a referee, and slowly turns toward the audience as ——

—— the CURTAIN *falls*

FURNITURE AND PROPERTY LIST

On stage: Wardrobe R. *On top*: Spare blankets concealing a video camera
Double bed diagonal from UR. *On it:* bedding and coverlet (for **Howard**)
Bedside cabinet on either side of bed, R cabinet with built-in radio, phone, bedside lamp, L cabinet with bedside lamp.
Small table
Chair UL
Chair DL

Off stage: Black sports holdall containing referee's shorts, shirt, socks, trainers, wallet with two photos (**Howard**)
Tray containing pot of tea, two cups, plates, knives, teaspoons, milk, jam, butter, muffins, bottle of pills (**Yellena**)

Personal: **Yellena**: small notebook and pencil, photo.

LIGHTING PLOT

Interior. The same scene throughout

To open: Room lit only by sliver of daylight diagonally across bed

Cue 1   **Yellena** opens curtains   (Page 1)
            Room filled with daylight

EFFECTS PLOT

Cue 1　To open　(Page 1)
Radio playing something Eastern European

Cue 2　**Yellena** switches off the radio　(Page 1)
Snap off radio

www.ingramcontent.com/pod-product-compliance
Lightning Source LLC
Chambersburg PA
CBHW070454050426
42450CB00012B/3271